# WORKBOOK

# KINGDOM HEROES

## TONY EVANS

**HARVEST HOUSE PUBLISHERS**
EUGENE, OREGON

Unless otherwise indicated, all Scripture quotations are taken from the New American Standard Bible®, © 1960, 1962, 1963, 1968, 1971, 1972, 1973, 1975, 1977, 1995 by The Lockman Foundation. Used by permission. (www.Lockman.org)

Cover design by Bryce Williamson

Cover photo © Keith Lance / Gettyimages

Interior design by KUHN Design Group

For bulk, special sales, or ministry purchases, please call 1-800-547-8979. Email: Customerservice@hhpbooks.com

**M** is a federally registered trademark of the Hawkins Children's LLC. Harvest House Publishers, Inc., is the exclusive licensee of the trademark.

**Kingdom Heroes Workbook**
Copyright © 2021 by Tony Evans
Published by Harvest House Publishers
Eugene, Oregon 97408
www.harvesthousepublishers.com

ISBN 978-0-7369-8408-9 (pbk.)
ISBN 978-0-7369-8409-6 (eBook)

**Printed in the United States of America**

21 22 23 24 25 26 27 28 29 /BP / 10 9 8 7 6 5 4 3 2 1

# CONTENTS

I want to thank my friends at Harvest House Publishers for their long-standing partnership in bringing my thoughts, studies, and words to print. I particularly want to thank Bob Hawkins for his friendship over the years as well as for his pursuit of excellence in leading his company. I also want to publicly thank Kim Moore for her help in the editorial process.

Working with the team at RightNow Media is always a pleasure, and they bring great professionalism and talent to what they do as well as a love for our Lord. Thank you, Phil Warner, for leading your group so well, and many thanks to the entire team that filmed and edited this study. In addition, my appreciation goes to Heather Hair for her skills and insights in collaboration on this Bible study content and assistance with the video production.

# MAKING THE MOST OF THIS WORKBOOK/PARTICIPANT'S GUIDE

This workbook and guide is a tool to help your group combine the video and subsequent Bible study into a dynamic growth experience. If you are the leader or facilitator of your group, take some time in advance to consider the questions in the Video Group Discussion and Group Bible Exploration sections of this guide, and then come up with personal examples to encourage discussion. Also make sure each individual has their own workbook, which will allow them to take notes during the group time as well as dig deeper on their own throughout the week.

Because every group session includes a video portion, think about the logistics. Before the session, ensure that everyone will be able to see the screen clearly and that the audio is set at a comfortable level. You don't want your group to miss anything.

Now let's preview the sections in each of the six sessions.

## Video Teaching Notes

Several key points and quotes from the video are provided in this section, and room to write notes is also provided.

## Video Group Discussion

Many of the discussion questions have to do with remembering what was just viewed, and this immediate follow-up is important; we can forget content unless we review it right away. Other questions in this section try to connect the video to emotions or experience: *How did you feel when Tony said that? Is that true in your life? Do you have the same issue?*

## Group Bible Exploration

This is a Bible study, so each session is grounded in Scripture. And because different levels of faith may be found within your group, this time in the Bible is to not only grow but to also help others find their faith.

## In Closing

The goal for every Bible study is to apply what's learned. This section highlights the main point of the session and challenges participants to dive deeper.

## On Your Own Between Sessions

This section includes additional study participants can do to keep the content they just learned fresh in their minds throughout the week and encourages them to put it into practice.

## Recommended Reading

Your group time will be enhanced if everyone reads the recommended chapters in *Kingdom Heroes* by Tony Evans before the next session. Tony's video teaching follows the book, but the book has considerably more information and illustrations. Everyone is encouraged to prepare ahead by reading the designated chapters.

# FAITH

Let's begin with Tony's definition of a kingdom hero: *A kingdom hero is a committed Christian who perseveres by faith in order to experience spiritual victory and divine approval.* Everything we're about to study aims at the goal of your living out your faith as a kingdom hero. By learning how others lived as kingdom heroes, you can apply what they did in their lives and the wisdom you gain from studying them to your own choices.

Here's an excerpt from *Kingdom Heroes*, focusing on what kingdom faith is:

> Faith isn't an amorphous concept or feeling you find in a faraway land. Nor is it merely an inclination. Kingdom faith means being absolutely sure of the things for which you hope. It involves living with the conviction of things you've not yet seen, a conviction that assures you they will come to pass. This conviction gives you the motivation and strength to endure when life becomes difficult. It gives you the hope to hang on to when sacrifices come into play with the pressures of a pagan or worldly culture.
>
> Faith deals with things that are real but haven't yet penetrated our five senses. Faith means actively functioning in the spiritual realm while simultaneously living in the physical realm.
>
> Now, keep in mind that faith is only as meaningful as the substance to which it is attached. Faith has to do with both an expectation and a hope because hope is an expectation about the future. If you have faith in a bad or unreliable substance, that faith won't produce anything. It's like a kid placing faith in the nonexistent tooth fairy. On her own, the tooth fairy won't do anything for that child because she isn't real. But because parents realize their children are placing faith in an unreal entity, they oftentimes leave a surprise under their children's pillows in place of a baby tooth that fell out.
>
> You can apply the same principle to Santa Claus. Santa, on his own, won't bring a single present to anyone, simply because he doesn't exist. But parents see the faith

of their children and respond in a way that reinforces that faith—they make surprise gifts appear under the Christmas tree.

Adults place faith in unreal concepts as well. It's just that, by and large, no one follows through on their misplaced faith, and many of them discover that life can come with significant disappointments. After choosing to place their faith in unreal concepts, they eventually learn that the way things turn out doesn't always resemble expectations.

A significant amount of faith placed in an insufficient substance will inevitably produce no results. That's because what makes faith demonstrable is the substance to which it is attached. If you want to grow your faith, you don't need to go faith-hunting. Rather, you need to focus on a better substance in which to place your faith. Make sure the substance is solid and real. Make sure your faith is in God and in Him alone.

*Kingdom Heroes*, pages 13-14

## Video Teaching Notes

As you watch the video, use the space on the next page to take notes. Some key points and quotes are provided as reminders.

## *Main Idea*

- At the beginning of any journey, we expect to one day finish—and in the life of a believer, the goal is to finish this life well and move on to eternity with Jesus. But what does getting there look like? This Bible study focuses on what it means to finish strong and why a life of faith will get us there.

- For many people, trying to finish what they've started—a side hustle, establishing a healthy diet, developing a consistent workout schedule—can prove to be discouraging.

- Whether because of difficulty, fear, or sheer exhaustion, giving up in the middle of a journey happens more frequently than we'd like to admit.

- This same desire to quit can occur in our spiritual lives if we don't have the faith to keep pushing in the race of life. But God has given us the opportunity to learn from men and women of the Bible whose faith allowed them to finish and finish well.

- By exploring their stories and heroic journeys of faith, we see how finishing well requires faith-filled living in every aspect of our lives and what it takes to make it to our end goal—all while keeping our eyes on Jesus Christ, the author and finisher of our faith.

- Personal Notes:

## Application

Faith is the foundation to successfully running and finishing the race of life.

## Quotables

- Not every Christian gets to be a kingdom hero. The fact that you're going to heaven comes from the free gift of eternal life, but to become a kingdom hero, you've got to take your confidence in God and live it out on earth.

- To live a life of faith, to have that your modus operandi, how you roll, is to act like God is telling the truth.

- Faith is acting like it is so even when it's not so, in order that it might be so simply because God said so.

## Video Group Discussion

1. In the video, Tony shares how the writer of Hebrews introduces each story of faith in chapter 11: with a phrase—*by faith*—and identifying who he's going to tell us about. Then he explains what that person did. Hebrews doesn't present faith as a theoretical or even a theological concept but rather as a practical way of living that enables believers to finish their race strong. In fact, each of these individuals finished strong enough to wind up in the Hall of Faith. How is finishing strong connected to the process of living a life by faith?

2. Tony compares faith in the tooth fairy or Santa Claus to the kind of faith that lacks substance; the two entities' lack of substance is tied to their lack of reality. Another translation

of the word *substance* is "assurance." Why is it important to view faith in light of the substance it's attached to—or in an attitude of "assurance"? What can we learn about the importance of where or in whom we place our faith from the opening verse of Hebrews 11: "Faith is the assurance of things hoped for, the conviction of things not seen"?

3. Below, read a passage referenced in the video, Hebrews 10:35-38, and reflect on its connection to living as a kingdom hero.

> Therefore, do not throw away your confidence, which has a great reward. For you have need of endurance, so that when you have done the will of God, you may receive what was promised. For yet in a very little while, He who is coming will come, and will not delay. But My righteous one shall live by faith; and if he shrinks back, My soul has no pleasure in him. But we are not of those who shrink back to destruction, but of those who have faith to the preserving of the soul.

**Reward.** Reflect specifically on verse 35: "Do not throw away your confidence, which has a great reward." How does this portion of the passage encourage us to stay committed in living a life of heroic kingdom impact?

**Promise.** Now reflect specifically on verse 36: "For you have need of endurance, so that when you have done the will of God, you may receive what was promised." Can you share a time when you felt like giving up, but you were able to endure and push forward because of the promises found in God's Word?

**Preservation.** Consider Hebrews 10:39: "We are not of those who shrink back to destruction, but of those who have faith to the preserving of the soul." The words *shrink back* reflect fear, doubt, and trepidation. Describe how these emotions can negatively impact a walk of faith.

How does knowing that God is assuring you of the preservation of your soul give you the courage not to shrink back in moments of fear?

4. In the video, Tony says, "You can be functioning by faith even when you aren't feeling faith-ish. Or you can feel faith-ish but not be living by faith because it didn't affect function." How does a person's function define their level of faith more than their feelings define it?

List two personal or hypothetical examples of feeling faith (without movement).

   1.

   2.

List two personal or hypothetical examples of functioning by faith (without feeling).

   1.

   2.

Once our feet start moving in steps of faith, we have demonstrated faith. On a scale of 1 to 10, rate the effectiveness of "feelings of faith" without any corresponding function.

1 ------------------------------------------------------------------- 10

Feelings of faith can often come out in our conversations, and they can even show up in our goals or notes as we study the Bible. But the true test of faith always shows up in our feet. It shows up by what we do, not by what we say. Share a specific way you can encourage yourself to move from feelings of faith into functions of faith this week.

## Group Bible Exploration

1. Read the following passages, then together explore and write down the various potential outcomes of living by faith.

   Mark 11:22-24—"[Jesus said to His disciples], 'Have faith in God. Truly I say to you, whoever says to this mountain, "Be taken up and cast into the sea," and does not doubt in his heart, but believes that what he says is going to happen, it will be granted him. Therefore I say to you, all things for which you pray and ask, believe that you have received them, and they will be granted you.'"

   Ephesians 2:8-9—"By grace you have been saved through faith; and that not of yourselves, it is the gift of God; not as a result of works, so that no one may boast."

1 John 5:4—"Whatever is born of God overcomes the world; and this is the victory that has overcome the world—our faith."

2. Matthew 14:22-33 tells about a time when the disciples were on their boat on the Sea of Galilee and a big storm arose. In the midst of the crashing waves and blowing wind they could see Jesus walking on the water toward them. All of the disciples saw Jesus and believed His faith enabled Him to walk on the water. They witnessed Him do it before their very eyes. But only one disciple chose to step out in his own faith and walk on the water himself—Peter. He wanted more than just witnessing Jesus' faith; he wanted to live out his own faith. As long as Peter kept his faith focused on the integrity of Jesus Christ, he stayed above the water. But when he began to focus on the storm, he began to sink.

Read Galatians 2:20—"I have been crucified with Christ; and it is no longer I who live, but Christ lives in me; and the life which I now live in the flesh I live by faith in the Son of God, who loved me and gave Himself up for me."

According to this verse, what is the correlation between fixing your faith on Christ and the fulfillment of the faith vision you hold?

Read James 1:6—"He must ask in faith without any doubting, for the one who doubts is like the surf of the sea, driven and tossed by the wind."

According to this verse, what does doubt do to the strength of a person's faith and to the fulfillment of the faith vision being held?

3. Read 1 Peter 1:7: "The proof of your faith, being more precious than gold which is perishable, even though tested by fire, may be found to result in praise and glory and honor at the revelation of Jesus Christ." In what ways do praise for, glory to, and honor of Jesus result from a life of heroic faith?

How would you feel if someone said they had faith that what you told them was true but their actions demonstrated the complete opposite?

Do you think God ever feels that way about you or others in the body of Christ? Why or why not?

## In Closing

As you end the study today, share prayer requests related to your quest to learn about kingdom heroes and live as one. Be specific about the areas you feel you most need to grow in and develop. Ask the Holy Spirit to open your heart throughout this study so you can live out your faith like never before. Also ask Him to guard and protect your priorities, time, and passions to enable you to finish this study in its entirety.

Before session 2, complete the "On Your Own Between Sessions" section below.

## On Your Own Between Sessions

1. In the book (page 18), Tony goes into greater detail about what it means to live by faith as a kingdom hero. He writes,

To live as a kingdom hero and be qualified for enshrinement in this hall is acting in alignment in faith under God. It means making choices in the physical realm based on what we cannot see but know to be true in the spiritual realm. The author of Hebrews reminds us of this in Hebrews 11:3: "By faith we understand that the worlds were prepared by the word of God, so that what is seen was not made out of things which are visible." Even the word *faith* itself came about through the activity of faith. God spoke into the invisible, and as a result, He created the visible. What we see now was made out of what we cannot see. The entire universe was created by One we cannot see while using things we cannot see in order to bring about what we can see.

Read these two Scripture passages:

John 1:18—"No one has seen God at any time; the only begotten God who is in the bosom of the Father, He has explained Him."

Colossians 1:15-16—"He is the image of the invisible God, the firstborn of all creation. For by Him all things were created, both in the heavens and on earth, visible and invisible, whether thrones or dominions or rulers or authorities—all things have been created through Him and for Him."

Knowing Jesus helps us to know God because He is the physical reflection of the invisible God. Why is it important to know Jesus personally, and how does that impact your ability to walk by faith?

What are some things that might distract you from drawing close to Jesus in such a way that builds your faith in Him and in the confidence of God Himself and His Word?

What can you do to lessen these distractions?

2. Anyone can finish something, but finishing well requires both having the faith that God will see you through the journey and committing to what it takes to finish well. Finishing is nothing new; we're all expected to finish things. Our boss requires us to finish our work. If we're an athlete, our coach requires us to finish our workout. The IRS requires us to finish our taxes. In a similar way, God requires us to finish our spiritual race with faith, worship, obedience, and courage. But finishing is much different from finishing strong. Read 1 Corinthians 9:24-27 and then reflect on the questions following.

> Do you not know that those who run in a race all run, but only one receives the prize? Run in such a way that you may win. Everyone who competes in the games exercises self-control in all things. They then do it to receive a perishable wreath, but we an imperishable. Therefore I run in such a way, as not without aim; I box in such a way, as not beating the air; but I discipline my body and make it my slave, so that, after I have preached to others, I myself will not be disqualified.

What is the difference between finishing first in a race and finishing last? Does finishing first have benefits?

According to this passage, does God want us to finish our life on earth just to finish? Or does He want us to finish in such a way that we "win"?

What does it mean to "win" in the Christian experience? (Note: Paul refers to this as an "imperishable" wreath.)

3. If you're going to finish the Christian life well as a kingdom hero, you have to understand God's grace and His standards in the process of getting there. Finishing well requires walking with God on His track, not God walking with you on yours. Tapping into God's grace enables you to find the endurance you need to finish well, like the kingdom heroes we're studying did. Read 1 Corinthians 15:10 and then paraphrase it in your own words: "But by the grace of God I am what I am, and His grace toward me did not prove vain; but I labored even more than all of them, yet not I, but the grace of God with me."

God desires your focus. He desires your faith. How does it make you feel to know He longs for your focus on and faith in Him so much that He will give you the grace you need in order to give them?

Ask God to enlighten your heart in order to see more clearly any areas of focus that are distracting you from living your life in full faith as a kingdom hero. Seek His heart and wisdom on how to retrain your focus to the pursuit of heroic, faith-filled living.

4. Life Exercise: Increasing Your Faith Steps

   *Identify* a time when you can spend concentrated and focused energy on talking with God about specific faith steps He wants you to take.

   *Consider* several ways you can put these faith steps into action.

   *Evaluate* how well you put these faith steps into action and what the results of stepping out in faith will be.

*Repeat* in the weeks to come. Incorporate the various aspects we're studying about living as a kingdom hero into your daily intimate time with God.

## Recommended Reading

In preparation for session 2, please read chapter 2 in *Kingdom Heroes* by Tony Evans.

# WORSHIP

Here's an excerpt from *Kingdom Heroes*, focusing on authentic worship:

A lot of people struggle with emotional instability in our contemporary society. In fact, never has there been a period when so much anxiety, depression, despair, and pain inflected a culture at the level they do now. Large numbers of people are depressed all the time, discouraged all the time, ticked off all the time, frustrated all the time, and can't seem to get along with anyone. They're just off—all the time.

Psychiatrists try to drug us out of depression. Entertainers try to distract us out of sadness. Self-help gurus seek to calm us out of our internal chaos. But until the root cause of all of that is acknowledged and addressed, much of the emotional turmoil plaguing us will remain. There are times when the root cause exists in deep personal loss or difficulty such as grief, as I know all too well. There are also times when the root cause may be found in a chemical imbalance or past traumatic experiences. In these situations, seeking professional help is essential. But there are other times when the root cause is separation from God through an avoidance of dealing with our sin through the grace and mercy of Jesus Christ and presenting our lives as a living sacrifice of worship. It is in those times that no amount of medication or distraction will be effective until the gap between a person and God is addressed.

Cheap worship produces cheap results. If you give God junk, don't be surprised if your emotions reflect junk as well. A great God deserves great honor and worship through your prioritization of His will and His ways in your everyday decisions. Authentic, all-consuming worship ushers in God's favor. A lack of sacrificial worship comes with its own consequences as well.

Zechariah 14:16-19 explains it this way:

Then it will come about that any who are left of all the nations that went against Jerusalem will go up from year to year to worship the King, the Lord of hosts, and to celebrate the Feast of Booths. And it will be that whichever of the families of the earth does not go up to Jerusalem to worship the King, the Lord of hosts, there will be no rain on them. If the family of Egypt does not go up or enter, then no rain will fall on them; it will be the plague with which the Lord smites the nations who do not go up to celebrate the Feast of Booths. This will be the punishment of Egypt, and the punishment of all the nations who do not go up to celebrate the Feast of Booths.

Many individuals fail to take God's Word and the precepts He attaches to His covenantal blessings, provision, and favor seriously, so they continue to live in a state of emptiness and emotional turmoil.

Worship is the starting point for your living as a kingdom hero, because without God's presence and access to His power in your life, you'll lack the stability and strength you need to regularly make heroic choices.

*Kingdom Heroes*, pages 33–35

## Video Teaching Notes

As you watch the video, use the space on the next page to take notes. Some key points and quotes are provided as reminders.

## *Main Idea*

- Finishing strong requires authentic worship throughout the race of life. Inauthentic worship shows us what we truly trust in, which will only lead us off the correct path. This session focuses on how important our worship is when living by faith.

- Abel offered God authentic worship by sacrificing from his best livestock, and in doing so, he acknowledged his sin. Authentic worship includes repentance.

- Abel worshipped God in an acceptable format because he based it on God's standards, not on his own.

- We are to be passionate about our worship, but we are also to be humble. We must worship God based on what He desires, not on what makes us feel good. Cain did the opposite of Abel; he worshipped with what made him feel good. As a result, he created a chain reaction of outcomes based on false religion. False religion is coming to God as we please, not as He requires.

- We are to worship God through more than Sunday morning services. We worship in how we work, in our relationships, in the stewardship of our body and our health, in how we choose to spend our free time, and more.

- Personal Notes:

## Application

Worshipping by faith requires believing in God, knowing God, and adjusting our expectations to His. Authentic worship displays an honest faith and trust in God. Are you giving God your leftovers? Or are you giving Him the very best you have to offer?

## Quotables

- Worship is the recognition of God for who He is, what He has done, and what we're trusting Him to do.

- You cannot bring to God what you want Him to have and skip what He wants you to give Him. He wants you to give Him what He has required.

- The Bible calls the worship of a Cain in Jude verse 11 the "way of Cain." Let me tell you what the way of Cain is. It's worshipping God by human reason, not worshipping God by divine revelation.

## Video Group Discussion

1. Tony begins this video session with an illustration about taking his kids to Universal Studios and walking through the façade of cities, buildings, and landscapes. He explains the comparison between the theme park and a believer's worship by saying, "When it comes to worship, a lot of people's worship is a façade. It looks authentic and real, but behind it there is no reality. It just has the face of worship." On a scale of 1 to 10, where are you in giving God authentic worship as opposed to giving Him just a façade (with 10 being authentic and 1 being a façade)?

1 ------------------------------------------------------------------ 10

2. In what ways does "cultural Christianity" potentially hinder giving God authentic worship?

3. What are some things that keep you from personally giving God authentic worship? (Examples might be distractions or a lack of interest.)

4. In what ways can you help yourself focus more on giving God authentic worship as opposed to giving Him just a façade?

5. In the video, Tony gives the illustration of a doctor writing a prescription for a sick person and the pharmacist interpreting the writing to fill the prescription. Tony mentions that if we were to write our own prescriptions without the medical knowledge necessary, pharmacists wouldn't fulfill them. And even if they did, the medicines wouldn't work because they wouldn't be what the doctor ordered.

Describe how believers sometimes write their own ways for how to worship God according to what they want, not based on Scripture.

On another scale from 1 to 10, where would you rate your own worship of God compared to what He has prescribed in His Word (1 being "your prescription" and 10 being "God's inherent Word")?

1 ---------------------------------------------------------------- 10

Describe any parallels or contrasts between your answers on the two scales (questions #1 and #5).

6. Identify how a greater level of authentic worship based on God's standards and not on your own can empower you to grow in your relationship with Him, receive His favor, and pursue your purpose more fully.

## Group Bible Exploration

1. Giving God worship does not necessarily translate into giving Him authentic worship. We see this laid out for us in the story of Cain and Abel. Cain brought something to God based on his own experiences and interests. Abel brought what God wanted and expected. Both brought something, but God accepted only one of the offerings. We discover this truth in Genesis 4:3-5: "Cain brought an offering to the LORD of the fruit of the ground. Abel, on his part also brought of the firstlings of his flock and of their fat portions. And the LORD had regard for Abel and for his offering; but for Cain and for his offering He had no regard."

Cain and Abel both knew what to do but only Abel chose to do it. Cain made a choice according to his own way of thinking. Why do you think Cain chose to give God what he did?

How do you feel when you see someone who claims to be a believer choosing to serve and worship God on their own terms rather than according to Scripture? Share why you think you feel the way you do.

How do you think it makes God feel if you or others choose to worship Him inauthentically—or even worse, just for show?

2. Compare and contrast the two *if* statements in Genesis 4:7:

First statement: "If you do well, will not your countenance be lifted up?"

Second statement: "If you do not do well, sin is crouching at the door; and its desire is for you, but you must master it."

What change of outcome does God give for worship done well versus worship not done well?

Describe how the principle found in Genesis 4:7 relates to a person's emotional state of mind.

American culture is at an all-time high for mental and emotional disorders, and yet God clearly gives us the cause-and-effect nature of worshipping Him and a person's emotional well-being. What is one way this solution step to greater mental health could be introduced into culture more clearly?

3. Worshipping God authentically requires intentionality and surrender to His prescribed ways. It also produces visible change in a person's countenance and emotional well-being. Worshipping God authentically may involve sacrificing the very best we have to offer, but in all of these experiences, worshipping Him raises people up so they can live as a kingdom hero. How? By causing them to be more spiritually and emotionally mature, which is then manifest in daily character traits.

Listed below are five character qualities that mark a kingdom hero in today's world along with a correlating Scripture. Identify an opposite or opposing emotion or quality for each one, then write it in the blank.

*Helpfulness*

Romans 15:1-2—"We who are strong ought to bear the weaknesses of those without strength and not just please ourselves. Each of us is to please his neighbor for his good, to his edification."

_____

*Consistency*

1 Corinthians 15:58—"My beloved brethren, be steadfast, immovable, always abounding in the work of the Lord, knowing that your toil is not in vain in the Lord."

_____

*Relational Commitment*

2 Kings 2:2—"Elijah said to Elisha, 'Stay here please, for the LORD has sent me as far as Bethel.' But Elisha said, 'As the LORD lives and as you yourself live, I will not leave you.' So they went down to Bethel."

_____

*Courage*

Deuteronomy 31:6—"Be strong and courageous, do not be afraid or tremble at them, for the LORD your God is the one who goes with you. He will not fail you or forsake you."

_____

*Honesty*

Proverbs 12:22—"Lying lips are an abomination to the LORD, but those who deal faithfully are His delight."

_____

Which qualities give you more real power to pursue your goals, contentment, and calling—the kingdom hero qualities or the opposite qualities? How so?

Why do you think very few people draw a connection between their worship of God and their ability to fully live out the victorious Christian life—even though it's clearly articulated and illustrated in Scripture?

4. Read together Malachi 1:7-10 and reflect on the discussion starters following:

> You are presenting defiled food upon My altar. But you say, "How have we defiled You?" In that you say, "The table of the LORD is to be despised." But when you present the blind for sacrifice, is it not evil? And when you present the lame and sick, is it not evil? Why not offer it to your governor? Would he be pleased with you? Or would he receive you kindly?" says the LORD of hosts. "But now will you not entreat God's favor, that He may be gracious to us? With such an offering on your part, will He receive any of you kindly?" says the LORD of hosts. "Oh that there were one among you who would shut the gates, that you might not uselessly kindle fire on My altar! I am not pleased with you," says the LORD of hosts, "nor will I accept an offering from you."

This passage gives us a glimpse into how strongly God feels about the kind of worship we bring Him. How do you think people's lives could improve if they started taking the worship of God more seriously?

Why is it important to realize the connection between how you worship God and the realities you face in your everyday life?

What often happens when we seek to worship according to our own level of interest or standards?

Malachi 1:7-10 makes the connection between what a person is willing to bring their governor and what they're willing to bring God. In today's culture this may be compared to what people are willing to give to themselves versus what they're willing to give to God. Based on these verses, describe how putting yourself first in your efforts, offerings, and purchases is counterintuitive to the goal of positioning yourself for personal growth and impact.

## In Closing

As you end the study today, pray together for a greater understanding of how worshipping God according to His prescribed ways actually empowers us in our everyday lives. Ask God for the wisdom and maturity to learn how to worship Him according to what pleases Him rather than what pleases us or signals virtue to others. Talk about ways you can encourage or remind each other to worship God more genuinely as part of your daily lives.

Before session 3, complete the "On Your Own Between Sessions" section below. You might want to start the next session with participants sharing what they learned from the exercises on those pages.

## On Your Own Between Sessions

1. Read the following three verses:

   John 4:24—"God is spirit, and those who worship Him must worship in spirit and truth."

   Romans 12:1—"I urge you, brethren, by the mercies of God, to present your bodies a living and holy sacrifice, acceptable to God, which is your spiritual service of worship."

   Hebrews 12:28—"Since we receive a kingdom which cannot be shaken, let us show gratitude, by which we may offer to God an acceptable service with reverence and awe."

   What do these verses tell you about the importance of worshipping God throughout your life and not just at designated times?

Based on these verses, list five ways we can worship God besides in church or with song.

1.

2.

3.

4.

5.

What changes can you make in your mindset or schedule to allow you more opportunities to worship God throughout your everyday life?

2. Read these two passages and then answer the questions following:

Exodus 34:14—"You shall not worship any other god, for the LORD, whose name is Jealous, is a jealous God."

Isaiah 29:13-14—"Then the Lord said, 'Because this people draw near with their words and honor Me with their lip service, but they remove their hearts far from Me, and their reverence for Me consists of tradition learned by rote, therefore behold, I will once again deal marvelously with this people, wondrously marvelous; and the wisdom of their wise men will perish, and the discernment of their discerning men will be concealed.'"

In what ways has our contemporary culture experienced a lessening of wisdom and discernment, if at all?

Describe your thoughts on the correlation between cultural, church, and familial devolution and a lack of authentic worship from the Christian collective.

What can you expect as potential outcomes for continuing to reduce an emphasis within churches today on what true worship is and the importance of it in relationship to all other things a person experiences in life?

3. Life Exercise: Examine Yourself

This week, read this excerpt from the book *Kingdom Heroes* once or twice a day. Meditate on different aspects of what Tony is asking you to consider, evaluate, and then do. Take time to write down your thoughts in response to this daily reading.

Before we continue our journey, I want you to do a mini self-audit. Ask yourself if you're giving God the time, talents, and treasures He seeks from you. Are you giving Him the first fruits of your energy, thoughts, heart, and soul? Or are you just tossing Him some Froot Loops here or there? You know, the interesting thing about Froot Loops is that, although they come in a bunch of different colors, they all taste the same. No matter what its color, every piece has the same flavor because they're all made from the same stuff.

I don't care what you toss to God or what fancy "color" it is, if it's not what He requires, it all tastes the same to Him. It's unacceptable worship, according to the One who matters most. Yet if you will give Him the worship He requires, your emotions will begin to heal. They will get stronger, more stable. You'll gain access to insights and wisdom you didn't have before. What's more, sin will have to stay behind the door because it won't have any negative energy to piggyback on. As a result, you won't wind up making bad choices, which bring about bad consequences only to leave a lasting legacy of shame.

*Kingdom Heroes*, page 38

Consider talking about the thoughts you wrote down when you gather with your group for the next session.

## Recommended Reading

In preparation for session 3, please read chapters 3–4 in *Kingdom Heroes* by Tony Evans.

# OBEDIENCE

Here's another excerpt from *Kingdom Heroes*, this one focusing on obedience through works and beginning with a Scripture passage from the book of James:

> What use is it, my brethren, if someone says he has faith but he has no works? Can that faith save him? If a brother or sister is without clothing and in need of daily food, and one of you says to them, "Go in peace, be warmed and be filled," and yet you do not give them what is necessary for their body, what use is that? Even so faith, if it has no works, is dead, being by itself (James 2:14-17).

James lets us know a faith that produces nothing at all exists. It is not active. It doesn't work. It's dried out. But he also lets us know how to reactivate faith—by combining what we do with what we believe. That brings it to life again. The work of obedience ignites the reality of faith so we see the invisible spiritual power enter into the visible reality around us.

This truth is tied to what we read earlier in Hebrews 11:1: "Faith is the assurance of things hoped for, the conviction of things not seen." Conviction always produces action. Convictions inform and inspire what we do, not just how we feel. Yet because so few Christians today live with much conviction at all, we're no longer seeing God operate through the body of Christ as He once did.

Similarly, believers are limiting God's miraculous intervention in their lives because they're trying to live with a dried-up, shriveled spirit. Yes, they may be saved and on their way to heaven, but they fail to witness heaven joining them on earth simply because God can't get them to work out their faith through actions. For faith to be real, it must be tied to something tangible you do.

Now remember, faith is not founded on what you feel. You can feel no faith at all but still be full of faith if you act in obedience to God based on what He says. Similarly, you can feel like you're full of faith and yet have no faith because you choose not to step out and move forward on what you've been shown to do. Walking by faith always involves movement. Without movement, there is no faith. You can shout, clap, holler, and even flip a pew in faith if you want to, and yet you'll have no living faith if you don't obey what God has revealed for you to do. If your feet don't move, your faith is dead.

We're facing an epidemic of indecisiveness in our culture today. So many people are simply afraid to make a decision. And the concept of groupthink has taken on a whole new meaning to such a degree that it's become a choke hold. Far too many of us wait for consensus from everyone and their brother and their cousin before moving ahead on anything. The existence of "cancel culture" has played into this fear of decision making. As a result, more often than ever, we as believers fail to move forward based on what God has directed us to do.

Just think about what would have happened if Noah had waited for consensus on building the ark. None of us would be here today. He would not have built the ark. When the floods came, the entire population would have been wiped out. Game over.

*Kingdom Heroes*, pages 58-59

## Video Teaching Notes

As you watch the video, use the space on the next page to take notes. Some key points and quotes are provided as reminders.

## *Main Idea*

- Living as a kingdom hero requires obedience. Part of our faith journey is relying on the wisdom of God in a world that goes against His Word. This session focuses on what it means to obey God and how it affects our living by faith.

- Noah acted on what he believed God said, revealing a living illustration of James 2:17, which states that faith without works is a dead faith. Noah lived as a kingdom hero because he chose obedience in the midst of challenge.

- To follow Noah's example, believers must push through the feelings of being uncomfortable in the culture. We are not to allow the chaotic environment to dictate our level of obedience to what God says to do.

- Having the faith to obey God when other options are out there is a true test [...] kingdom living. Decisions made based on fear or peer pressure are not ma[...] obedience to God. Choices made in faith, which produce obedience, is what [...] person toward the hall of kingdom heroes.

- Personal Notes:

## Application

Choose to believe God's plan and act on it despite what the culture is saying, doing, or even pressuring you to do.

## Quotables

- The culture doesn't have to define you. The culture doesn't have to dictate to you. The culture doesn't have to direct you. You can choose to be the odd-person-out in the culture. Why? Because you want divine favor.

- God's Word is not just words about God. It is the voice of God in print that He expects us to respond to—watch this, even when it doesn't make sense.

- Faith is believing what you cannot yet empirically see.

## Video Group Discussion

1. In the video, Tony begins by describing what Noah did and the cultural context in which he did it. He explains that God has emotions, and when He examined the earth and all of the sinfulness upon it—as well as the demonic infiltration—it made Him sad (Genesis 6:6). God's emotional side is often overlooked. What are some things we can learn about God through this insight into His emotions?

2. While the debauchery of the culture made God grieve, Moses' obedience and right living appealed to God's emotions. As a result, He showed Moses favor (Genesis 6:8). How significant is God's favor in a person's life, in practical terms? Share some examples of God's favor in your or others' lives.

How should knowing the importance of having God's favor on your life and productivity as a kingdom hero affect your everyday decision-making related to your interaction with God?

3. Tony brought up "cancel culture"* in this video session, urging believers to not worry about being canceled by the culture but rather worry about being canceled by Christ. Of course, he wasn't referring to salvation but to Christ's favor in a person's life and what that favor can produce. Describe your reaction to contemporary society's "cancel culture" and how that affects people's decisions and words today.

What would believers' lives look like, or how might they change, if they worried more about Jesus canceling His favor over them versus the culture's sway and pressure?

---

* From *Merriam-Webster's Collegiate Dictionary*, 11th edition: "*Cancel culture* [has] to do with the removing of support for public figures in response to their objectionable behavior or opinions. This can include boycotts or refusal to promote their work." Of course, the behavior and opinions are objectionable as they are *perceived* to be.

One could say that the flood was the largest demonstration of "cancel culture." In light of God's power, should the world take Him more seriously than it does? Why?

4. What are some ways you can change your decisions or what you say in order to appeal more directly to God's favor?

5. What prominent principle stood out to you from the video teaching for this session? Share why it affected you and how it motivated you to live as a kingdom hero.

## Group Bible Exploration

1. Read together 1 Peter 3:18-20:

> Christ also died for sins once for all, the just for the unjust, so that He might bring us to God, having been put to death in the flesh, but made alive in the spirit; in which also He went and made proclamation to the spirits now in prison, who once were disobedient, when the patience of God kept waiting in the days of Noah, during the construction of the ark, in which a few, that is, eight persons, were brought safely through the water.

Explain the connection between the patience of God and our salvation, which is both temporal through life's challenges and eternal.

Contrast the phrase *put to death in the flesh* with the phrase *made alive in the spirit.*

2. Read these Scripture passages together:

> If you are living according to the flesh, you must die; but if by the Spirit you are putting to death the deeds of the body, you will live (Romans 8:13).

> Consider the members of your earthly body as dead to immorality, impurity, passion, evil desire, and greed, which amounts to idolatry. For it is because of these things that the wrath of God will come upon the sons of disobedience, and in them you also once walked, when you were living in them. But now you also, put them all aside: anger, wrath, malice, slander, and abusive speech from your mouth. Do not lie to one another, since you laid aside the old self with its evil practices, and have put on the new self who is being renewed to a true knowledge according to the image of the One who created him (Colossians 3:5-10).

Describe the correlation and similarities between these two passages.

In what practical ways ought *putting to death the flesh* show up in our everyday thoughts, words, and actions?

How critical is it for kingdom followers to model their own behavior after Jesus Christ in putting to death the flesh and its desires so they can be made alive in the Spirit? Be specific and explain why.

3. Tony references James 2 when talking about the importance of demonstrating the viability of faith through works, actions, and obedience. Read James 2:14-26 together and then discuss the questions following:

> What use is it, my brethren, if someone says he has faith but he has no works? Can that faith save him? If a brother or sister is without clothing and in need of daily food, and one of you says to them, "Go in peace, be warmed and be filled," and yet you do not give them what is necessary for their body, what use is that? Even so faith, if it has no works, is dead, being by itself. But someone may well say, "You have faith and I have works; show me your faith without the works, and I will show you my faith by my works." You believe that God is one. You do well; the demons also believe, and shudder.
>
> But are you willing to recognize, you foolish fellow, that faith without works is useless? Was not Abraham our father justified by works when he offered up Isaac his son on the altar? You see that faith was working with his works, and as a result of the works, faith was perfected; and the Scripture was fulfilled which says, "And Abraham believed God, and it was reckoned to him as righteousness," and he was called the friend of God. You see that a man is justified by works and not by faith alone. In the same way, was not Rahab the harlot also justified by works when she received the messengers and sent them out by another way? For just as the body without the spirit is dead, so also faith without works is dead.

Based on the video teaching and this passage, what does faith without accompanying works (actions) accomplish for a believer?

What does this passage mean when it speaks of faith being "perfected" through works?

God reckoned Abraham as righteous on what accord?

If you ordered a meal at a restaurant and the waiter brought you empty plates, how would that make you feel? What would that say about the waiter, the cooks, and the restaurant establishment?

How do you think God feels when we say we have faith but don't back it with our actions? What does that say about us?

## In Closing

As you end the study today, pray together for a greater willingness to relinquish the desires of the flesh and pursue obedience to God through the power of Christ and His Spirit. Ask God for insight and a greater motivation on your part to follow Him in all things.

Before session 4, complete the "On Your Own Between Sessions" section below.

## On Your Own Between Sessions

1. Chapter 4 in *Kingdom Heroes,* pages 57-58, says,

   > Many of us fail to live our lives as kingdom heroes simply because our faith has dried up. We go through the motions only to discover that our Christian walk has gone flat. We talk about believing in God, but the power has fizzled. The luster has been lost. The shine has dimmed to a flicker. When the faith we need to fully experience the victory of kingdom living has faded and fallen to the wayside, heroic actions to advance God's kingdom remain dormant within.

   Tony then goes on to talk about James 2:14-17, which we looked at in the "Group Bible Exploration." You may want to reread this passage on your own in preparation for these questions.

   What does it mean to say that faith without works is dead?

What are some ways to activate a dormant level of faith?

What specific step can you take this week to activate your faith on a greater scale?

2. Read Matthew 25:34-40:

> Then the King will say to those on His right, "Come, you who are blessed of My Father, inherit the kingdom prepared for you from the foundation of the world. For I was hungry, and you gave Me something to eat; I was thirsty, and you gave Me something to drink; I was a stranger, and you invited Me in; naked, and you clothed Me; I was sick, and you visited Me; I was in prison, and you came to Me." Then the righteous will answer Him, "Lord, when did we see You hungry, and feed You, or thirsty, and give You something to drink? And when did we see You a stranger, and invite You in, or naked, and clothe You? When did we see You sick, or in prison, and come to You?" The King will answer and say to them, "Truly I say to you, to the extent that you did it to one of these brothers of Mine, *even* the least *of them*, you did it to Me."

What is one of the primary ways of living as a kingdom hero?

What are some things you can do to help improve other people's lives in a tangible manner?

Based on this passage, how should faith in Jesus and your love for Him connect with service to others?

3. Read Matthew 5:16—"Let your light shine before men in such a way that they may see your good works, and glorify your Father who is in heaven." What is the intended result of doing good works based in faith?

Describe the phrase *let your light shine* in your own words as it pertains to steps taken in faith.

Just as we're studying kingdom heroes from days gone by, people may one day look at your life as an example of heroic faith. What is one thing you would want them to think or say about your life?

4. Life Exercise: Participating in Your Walk of Faith

*Identify* one area where you need to focus on activating your faith so it leaves an impact on your life and the lives of those around you.

*Consider* how to fill your mind with what you need to build your faith, particularly related to an area where you can advance God's kingdom agenda in a more tangible way. Also ask God to give you specific interactions with people, His Word, sermons you listen to, books you read—anything that will inform your faith thoughts in order to do what you need to do to make a difference.

*Evaluate* ways to put your new awareness and confidence into faith-filled actions.

*Share,* if you feel led, what you've learned after taking steps of faith to begin making the greater impact you desire. Share with friends and family and on social media as well as with the other participants in this study.

## Recommended Reading

In preparation for session 4, please read chapters 5–9 in *Kingdom Heroes* by Tony Evans.

# WISDOM

ere's an excerpt from *Kingdom Heroes*, focusing on the importance of asking God for wisdom:

Moses knew the eternal award that awaited him in the hands of the one, true God would be much more meaningful than anything he might experience on this earth, no matter how fun it might be in the moment. He understood what truly mattered, which is why he made the choice he did. He picked a side.

But I don't think Moses was thinking only of an eternal reward. Again, we have to keep in mind that his mother's voice had been speaking to him since the time of his birth. She'd given him the history of the Hebrew people. She'd told him the stories of Abraham and the agreement he and God made—that one day there would be an entire nation. She shared with him the promise of a land and that someone would need to lead them there. We don't know for sure, but she probably told him he was the one to do so. After all, he'd been placed in the palace for such a time as this.

Moses' mother no doubt urged him not to settle for the junk of Egypt while missing out on the reward of God's promise for the Hebrew people. He was a leader. He was intelligent. He'd been spared and chosen by God Himself. I'm sure she didn't want her son to fall so in love with the world that he would miss out on God's plan for his life altogether, even though that's easy to do. People can fall so in love with secular society that they wind up dying with money in the bank, a big house, and a nice car but a wasted life because they never got around to experiencing God's plan for them.

The reward of God is greater than the treasures of man. But unless you believe that you won't make the wise decision like Moses did. You'll wind up hanging out with the world rather than giving yourself fully to God.

ıde up his mind as a result of his faith in both a reward to experience in
d an eternal one. Hebrews 11:27 explains it like this: "By faith he left
ıg the wrath of the king; for he endured, as seeing Him who is unseen."
ᴜ faith in choosing God's presence over the earthly king. Yet as I men-
ᴇarlier, he didn't necessarily think it through. By jumping out there to kill the
ᴇgyptian before making any clear headway in his relationship with the Hebrew people, he left not much more than confusion on the table and a bad taste in the mouths
of those he sought to help.

Through that graphic mistake, he wound up running for his life. His presump-
tive spirit led him on a detour that lasted for decades. While Moses assumed the
Hebrews would know he was acting as their deliverer, he made the mistake of not
checking with God first. He tried to do a good thing, but it ended up being a bad
thing altogether.

Yet God, despite Moses' wrong action, knew his heart and motive had been right.
That just didn't remove the consequence of his unwise choice.

*Kingdom Heroes*, pages 143-144

## Video Teaching Notes

As you watch the video, use the space on the next page to take notes. Some key points and
quotes are provided as reminders.

### Main Idea

- Living by faith includes consistently pursuing God's wisdom in order to differenti-
  ate between His standard and the world's standard. This will determine the way we're
  ultimately known and remembered as a kingdom hero. Our beliefs have a lot to do
  with the choices we make. We should walk in God's wisdom when making decisions,
  because when we do, our decisions will produce good results.

- Pursuing the wisdom of God is the only way to fully embody being a kingdom hero.

- The wisdom of the world gets us off track. God's wisdom leads us down the correct
  road.

- The life of Moses displays the importance of having discernment and striving for God's
  standard.

- Moses' parents chose God's plan over the culture's plan. If we're going to live as a kingdom hero, we can't allow ourselves to be distracted by what the world says.

- Moses grew up, and despite facing danger, he chose to honor his heritage and his God rather than the gods of Egypt.

- Personal Notes:

## Application

Your submission to God should push you to choose His wisdom over your own in your daily life.

## Quotables

- The way you know to make the right decisions is that you learn to live by faith in who God is and what God says, not just in what you think and how you feel at any given time.

- Far too many Christians are unwilling to be identified as a Christian outside of their convenient Christian environment.

- God is going to reward those believers—kingdom heroes—who decide that they don't mind being identified with Him.

## Video Group Discussion

1. Read together Hebrews 11:23—"By faith Moses, when he was born, was hidden for three months by his parents, because they saw he was a beautiful child; and they were not afraid of the king's edict." What does this passage say about Moses' parents' level of fear?

How did their lack of fear lead to a faith decision?

Is it possible to not live in a continual state of fear that impacts your decisions even when those in authority are making decisions to promote a culture of fear? If it is, what can help make it possible?

2. Read Hebrews 11:24-26 together—"By faith Moses, when he had grown up, refused to be called the son of Pharaoh's daughter, choosing rather to endure ill-treatment with the people of God than to enjoy the passing pleasures of sin, considering the reproach of Christ greater riches than the treasures of Egypt; for he was looking to the reward."

Describe a situation or time when you made choices based on an anticipation of a spiritual reward over a temporal and physical gain.

Do you believe God's rewards outweigh the pleasures of sin in the long run? Why or why not?

3. In the video, Tony uses the backdrop of Moses' choices to present a question to each of us. He asks, "Have you made the decision to no longer be an undefined voter? That you're standing flat-footed in midair or that you're no longer going to be identified sometimes as a follower of Christ and sometimes as comfortable in the culture?"

How do you answer this question, and why?

What actions have you taken or plan to take to support your answer to this question?

4. During the video, Tony shares about the intimate time when his late wife, Lois, was transitioning from the present reality on earth to heaven. She spoke of a reward they wanted to give her but they were just waiting for the music. This insight gave the Evans family comfort in a time of difficulty and pain. Have you ever experienced or read about a similar situation during the passing of a believer in Christ? If so, what did you learn from it?

What are some things that hinder us from keeping eternal rewards front and center in our hearts and minds?

What wisdom can we glean from recognizing the reality that God does have rewards for His faithful kingdom heroes? How can that wisdom impact our daily lives?

## Group Bible Exploration

1. Read these Scripture verses together:

Proverbs 1:5—"A wise man will hear and increase in learning, and a man of understanding will acquire wise counsel."

Proverbs 12:15—"The way of a fool is right in his own eyes, but a wise man is he who listens to counsel."

Based on these two verses, what is one way to gain wisdom?

What are some personal hindrances that keep people from pursuing the gaining of wisdom through others? (Examples: pride or isolation.)

How can we identify who would be considered "wise counsel"?

2. Now read together James 1:5—"If any of you lacks wisdom, let him ask of God, who gives to all generously and without reproach, and it will be given to him." What does it mean to ask God for wisdom?

How often should we ask for wisdom?

How can we discern between wisdom from God and our normal, everyday thoughts?

What are some dangers of leaning on our own understanding as opposed to asking God for wisdom and applying it?

3. Read together Joshua 1:9—"Have I not commanded you? Be strong and courageous! Do not tremble or be dismayed, for the LORD your God is with you wherever you go." The Bible connects God's presence with us—wherever we go—with our ability to remove fear and trembling from our life. How can we seek to identify the presence of God on a greater level in our everyday life?

Why do you think Joshua had to use the term *commanded* regarding telling the Israelites to be strong and not fear?

Fear is an emotion. What are some ways we can choose not to allow fear to have a negative impact on us and our choices?

4. Based on Proverbs 13:20—"He who walks with wise men will be wise, but the companion of fools will suffer harm"—what is a key element to living with wisdom?

What does it mean to "walk with wise men"?

On a scale of 1 to 10, where would you rate your current circle of relationships with regard to those people's level of spiritual wisdom?

1 ------------------------------------------------------------------ 10

Now, on a scale of 1 to 10, where would you rate your current circle of influencers (social media contacts, book authors, podcast speakers, and so on) with regard to their level of spiritual wisdom?

1 ------------------------------------------------------------------ 10

Do you see any room for improvement in whom you choose to surround you on a regular basis?

*Fool* is a harsh word, and we don't always say someone is a fool. But God doesn't mince words when He calls out those who choose to live by the world's standards rather than by His. God does this to warn us of the potential for harm that comes when surrounding ourselves with those whose choices reflect Satan's agenda, not God's. Fools can be well-known and even popular in culture, but the path they lead others on is one of destruction. Can you name any cultural groups whose messages are foolish against the backdrop of God's wisdom?

## In Closing

As you close your time together, encourage one another to let God's 'standard for all choices. Remind one another that there is only one to fear self. Take some time to encourage those in your group who may be strug cifically for anyone going through a crisis right now.

Before session 5, complete the "On Your Own Between Sessions" secti

## On Your Own between Sessions

1. In chapter 9 of *Kingdom Heroes* (pages 137-138), Tony tells us what he thinks is one reason Moses grew up to live a life of heroic faith. He writes,

   *Not afraid.* Those two words sum up how Moses grew to express such greatness. The parents who gave him life were "not afraid." They lived with faith over fear. The DNA passed down to their son through this genetic transfer was that of belief.

   But even more than that, Moses' parents' lack of fear in the face of an evil culture and evil king spared his life. They chose to hide him so he would not be killed, as the king of Egypt had mandated midwives do away with male Hebrew babies as soon as they were born. Then, when Moses had grown too old to hide, they came up with an elaborate scheme to position him in a safe and secure place. Looking at their plan as a strategist, you might even say they sought to infiltrate the system that oppressed them through this act of faith, in order to bring about a positive influence for good.

   Why is fear such a deterrent to living a life of faith?

   Knowing that fear can cripple someone from living out their purpose, do you think Satan intentionally seeks to create a "culture of fear" among humanity? If you do, what do you think are some of his approaches to accomplish this?

hat are some of your deepest, most authentic fears?

Take some time to pray about what you just wrote and ask God to give you the faith to overcome them, leaving them at His feet and casting your cares upon Him.

2. On the last page of chapter 9 in *Kingdom Heroes* (page 146), Tony writes,

You may identify with Moses in his impulsivity during his younger years. Or maybe with him in his insecurity in his older years. Whatever the case, Moses gives all of us an example of what it means to be redeemed from the frailties of our flesh and used by the power of God working in us. His story ought to inspire all of us to dream big as to what God can and will do through us for others.

List three dreams, goals, or aspirations you currently have or wish to one day pursue.

1.

2.

3.

Is anything from your past keeping you from pursuing one or more of the three things listed above? If so, what is it, and how can you let it go?

What can you do this week to take a step toward each of these three things listed?

3. Life Exercise: Unleash Faith over Fear

This week, intentionally face your fears in such a way that you overcome them with a victorious faith.

Spend some time meditating on the scriptural truths related to faith that are also related to forgiveness and God's grace. Satan will often seek to keep someone trapped in past shame or past trauma, which leads to a fear of future shame or future trauma. This keeps that person immobile.

As you continually look to God for His grace in your life, be sure to show yourself grace too. Allow yourself to grieve any past trauma you've experienced, and then let it go. Know that the past is not a predictor of the future. You can move forward in faith knowing that the God you follow is strong enough to protect you and guide you each step of the way.

## Recommended Reading

In preparation for session 5, please read chapter 10 in *Kingdom Heroes* by Tony Evans.

# RISK

H ere's an excerpt from *Kingdom Heroes*, this one focusing on risk:

The people we've seen in the Hall of Heroes all knew risk. They knew what it was like to put all of their eggs in God's basket. They went all in, and because they did, they reaped an eternal and oftentimes also an earthly reward. Faith is risky business. But it comes with the opportunity to gain a tremendous reward if you put your faith in that which is worthy of it—God.

A risk involves taking a chance on something without any empirical evidence for where it will wind up. You can't prove whatever it is will turn out like you hope, but you still decide to move forward with the hope that it will.

Faith always involves risk, and God wants you to take a risk on Him because He knows He's dependable. The Bible tells us He is. So even though He's invisible to your eyes, you have His written Word. And God regularly makes promises He wants you to act on before you see them worked out. He creates opportunities for you to take a risk on what He's said. Oftentimes, He does that by allowing a spiritual crisis in your life to occur.

Now, when I say spiritual crisis, I'm not talking about a normal trial or difficulty. Life comes with challenges just by its nature. That's not what I mean by a spiritual crisis. A spiritual crisis takes place when God puts you in a situation only He can fix. When He places you in a scenario you can't buy your way out of, negotiate your way out of, or find someone to get you out of it, you know this is a spiritual crisis. Essentially, God has boxed you in.

What's more, in a situation like this, if God doesn't come through for you, you're sunk.

That is exactly where the Israelites find themselves as we continue our walk through the Hall of Heroes. Either God is going to bail them out of their difficulties or they will drown under them—literally.

It's interesting to note that, at this point in the exhibits, we see a switch from a person to a people group. That's because the author of Hebrews does that. In the midst of individual hero descriptions, he switches to the Israelites. That reveals that not only is it critical for us to live with individual faith but to learn to live with collective faith as well. What we do as a people group, or as a body of kingdom followers, will impact us too.

What we do personally matters. But what we do collectively also matters. Sometimes we forget that one person's actions impact those around them, but the actions of a group of people leave an even larger ripple on the waters of our world events.

*Kingdom Heroes*, pages 149-151

## Video Teaching Notes

As you watch the video, use the space below to take notes. Some key points and quotes are provided as reminders.

### *Main Idea*

- Living as a kingdom hero requires you to take risks. The heroic Christian life is all about risk, because when you aren't living by sight, anything can happen to surprise you. This session focuses not only on why living by faith can be risky but on how it's worth the risk.

- Having faith can be a risk because we can't see God, nor can we see the things we're having faith for.

- Remember, it may be a risk to us, but it's always calculated by God.

- Walking by faith and not by sight is a risk that's guaranteed to get us closer to Jesus— our ultimate goal.

- The people of Israel had to display their faith in God through the blood on their doorposts. They had never heard that kind of instruction before, and it was risky to rely on it. Yet they took the risk to believe in something that didn't make sense to them, and they were rewarded for it—with their lives.

- Personal Notes:

## Application

You have to be willing to take the risk on God's Word to experience its worth.

## Quotables

- There is a risk to faith because you are dealing with something that you do not see in advance.

- Let me tell you when you know you are on your way to being a kingdom hero. When you are in a crisis and you have to bet on the Lord. When you are in a crisis and you have to take the risk of faith. When you are in a crisis and you have to believe God against all odds, especially when the odds are against you.

- Your past does not have to determine your future.

## Video Group Discussion

1. Tony opens this session talking about a scene in one of the films in the nostalgic Indiana Jones series, the one that involves the main character's pursuit of the Holy Grail. In order to find it, he has to take a risk. He has to take a step of faith. Most things of great value require risk.

   Have you ever taken a step of faith or a risk for something you perceived to be of great value? If so, share your experience and what you learned from it.

2. Read Luke 9:57-58—"As they were going along the road, someone said to Him, 'I will follow You wherever You go.' And Jesus said to him, 'The foxes have holes and the birds of the air have nests, but the Son of Man has nowhere to lay His head.'" What do these verses tell us about the difference between "feeling" like taking a step of faith and the "actual experience" of taking a step of faith?

3. In the video, Tony talks about how the things God asks us to do don't always make sense to us. What are some thoughts you think went through the Israelites' minds when they were asked to put the blood of a lamb on their doorposts in order to protect the lives of their firstborn males?

What types of things has God asked people to do in Scripture that involved a personal risk? List three practical examples.

   1.

   2.

   3.

In the video Tony mentioned that the miracle of the Red Sea actually involved two miracles. What were they?

   1.

   2.

Describe how you may have felt walking through the middle of the parted waters. What might you have said, done, or thought to calm your mind or increase your courage?

Take a moment to pray as a group, asking God to supply heroic, supernatural faith. Ask for this faith to take root in your hearts and bear fruit through your actions.

## Group Bible Exploration

1. Read Exodus 12:33-36 together:

The Egyptians urged the people, to send them out of the land in haste, for they said, "We will all be dead." So the people took their dough before it was leavened, with their kneading bowls bound up in the clothes on their shoulders. Now the sons of Israel had done according to the word of Moses, for they had requested from the Egyptians articles of silver and articles of gold, and clothing; and the LORD had given the people favor in the sight of the Egyptians, so that they let them have their request. Thus they plundered the Egyptians.

The Israelites' step of faith—putting the blood of a lamb on their doorposts before the death angel's visit on what came to be called Passover—made a tremendous statement on the hearts and minds of their captors. Why do you think their former captors now helped them on their way?

How can experiencing God's hand of favor as a result of our stepping out in faith impact the way other people treat us when they witness it?

2. Read these verses and then identify their connection to living with heroic, active faith:

   Romans 8:31—"What then shall we say to these things? If God is for us, who is against us?"

   Matthew 19:26—"Jesus said to them, 'With people this is impossible, but with God all things are possible.'"

   What is the source of our faith?

How can the truths of these two verses impact your daily decisions?

In chapter 9 of *Kingdom Heroes*, Tony tells about a time he encouraged his congregation to gather and pray for a parcel of land he thought for sure God was giving them. But the land went to a higher bidder. Tony compared this experience to the roller-coaster feelings the Israelites may have felt in leaving Egypt with the blessing of their captors only to be trapped at the Red Sea. Sometimes it seems like God delivers us only to set us up.

In the book *Kingdom Heroes* (page 157), Tony explains that a few years later, the church did acquire the land after all. Then he writes, "God doesn't always open our Red Seas or feed our five thousands or topple our giants right when we want Him to. That's why faith is so risky. We're not only relying on Him for His ability to pull things off but learning how to trust that He will do so at the right time, letting go of our own need for control."

Do you think it's possible to accurately hear what God says He's going to do but misinterpret the timing of His hand? If so, what are some possible results of that misinterpretation?

Has this ever happened to you or someone you know? If so, what did you or they learn?

3. Based on Matthew 6:34—"Do not worry about tomorrow; for tomorrow will care for itself. Each day has enough trouble of its own"—how does God ask us to view the timing of His plans?

Describe what it means to "not worry" in practical terms.

Can worry impact a person's decisions for how they spend their time? If so, how?

## In Closing

As you end this session today, consider the ways the roller coaster of our spiritual growth can impact our daily life. Share how letting go and trusting God and His timing can free up our emotions for more enjoyable things. Ask God to reveal an approach to letting go and trusting Him in faith to each person in the group that fits with their own style of life and personality.

Before session 6, complete the "On Your Own Between Sessions" section below.

## On Your Own Between Sessions

1. God desires for you to step out in risky moves of faith in order to experience His hand of deliverance. Each time He does, He develops a repertoire of faith-based memories to boost your courage for future action. We read about this in Psalm 77:11: "I shall remember the deeds of the LORD; surely I will remember Your wonders of old."

   List three "deeds" God has done in your life, coming through for you.

   1.

   2.

   3.

2. Life Exercise: Grow Your Faith Through the Word of God

One way to grow your faith is to connect with God's Word more regularly. Each day over the course of the next week, intentionally set aside time to read a specific passage dealing with faith (search online for recommended passages). Read the same passage every day for seven days. Each day before you read it, ask God to prepare your heart to hear from Him.

In a journal or on a smart device, write down the various insights God gives you each day. Revisiting the same passage every day for seven days gives you the opportunity to abide more fully in the written Word of God, increasing your ability to hear from Him regarding the meaning and application of His Word.

If you feel led, in next week's group session share what you learned and how it impacted your life.

3. Reflection: Taking a Risk Step

How can you take a risk step of faith this week?

Take some time to seriously consider this step, pray, feel, be convicted, and let the presence of God reveal where you can be more intentional about stepping out in faith. Do you need to integrate thoughts about active faith more into your day-to-day activities? If so, how do you plan to do that?

## Recommended Reading

In preparation for session 6, please read chapters 11–13 in *Kingdom Heroes* by Tony Evans.

# A TRIUMPHANT FINISH

ere's an excerpt from *Kingdom Heroes*, focusing on you and your faith journey:

The bottom line? We are not to lose heart.

Let me help you with a picture of what it means to lose heart. Losing heart is like runners becoming exhausted to the point of collapse. They lose all strength, energy, and even motivation to continue. To lose heart is to say, "Even though I want to go on, I just can't go any farther."

Now, most of us have known what that feels like at some point. For many of us, it's become the way of life itself. Weariness is the new normal. Losing heart is a day-in and day-out reality. But the author of Hebrews wants us to know it doesn't have to be that way. He's given us example after example of those who stood up against the dangers and difficulties of their time and kept going despite the hardships.

They did it. They made it to the Hall of Heroes. They didn't throw in the towel. They risked. They set out. They believed. They stood up. They made choices based on what they truly believed in. As a result, they lived out the definition of faith. Their decisions became the substance of things hoped for and the evidence of things unseen. They made the seemingly unreachable, reachable after all. They made it because of where they chose to focus...

Keep in mind, faith is only as powerful as the object or being it's placed in. Put your faith in the tooth fairy, and you won't wind up with much of worth. On the contrary, God is real. He's the object of our hope. If God were not real, then faith would be like grasping after air.

For example, you'll often hear sports teams or athletes make statements like "I believe," with a period at the end of that sentence. Well, believe in what? That's not a complete understanding of faith, because faith must include the substance. It must include the thing you're grabbing hold of. Belief in believing is never enough. Thus, the question of faith always comes down to the worth of the object in which you place your confidence.

Biblical faith isn't just a feeling. Neither is it an attitude or simply an insignia on your T-shirt or hat. It's more than a saying you post on social media. Biblical faith is grabbing hold of that which you cannot see in order to access the authority and activity of the One in whom you placed your faith. If your feet are still, and you are not moving, you don't have faith. You may have emotions, but only actions reveal true faith…

The author of Hebrews wanted to remind any of us who feel discouraged that persevering brings about a reward. Walking by faith ushers in a greater tomorrow. Even though things are tough, we're to maintain our Christian commitment through the vicissitudes and challenges of life.

Many of you may have grown up in the old church style, where as he preached the preacher would often ask, "Can I get a witness?" Or he might have said, "You have somebody who can testify!" In other words, he was reminding his listeners they weren't the first people to be where they were. Other people had gone through the fire and come out the other side unscathed. What's more, they could testify about it…

These individuals the author of Hebrews mentions went through the difficulties and trials of life in such a way that they stood approved before God in the end. They heard the "well done" statement. And, what's more, they remain as legacies of faith to serve as inspiration to all of us. This is how they are referred to at the start of Hebrews 12 where it says, "Since we have so great a cloud of witnesses…" Or if you want to put that in the context of the Hall of Heroes setting, you could say, "Since we have so great a number of kingdom heroes…" The reminder is simple. Since they made it, you can too. Since they prevailed, you can prevail. Since they found a way, there's a way for you as well.

*Kingdom Heroes*, pages 197-199

## Video Teaching Notes

As you watch the video, use the space on the next page to take notes. Some key points and quotes are provided as reminders.

## *Main Idea*

- A good understanding of what it takes to become a kingdom hero is important when we choose a life of faith. It's just as important to know that we have an example in

Jesus, the One who has gone before us, showing us the way of faith and how it looks to keep our eyes fixed on Him.

- Walking by faith can be difficult, but the Hall of Heroes can serve as an encouragement as we push to remain steadfast.

- We know this journey is possible due to the cloud of witnesses who persisted through faith before us.

- The race of life is all about seeing Jesus. Kingdom heroes keep their eyes fixed on Him.

- Faith and seeing Jesus go hand in hand. We must follow Jesus' example of looking past the pain and fixing our focus beyond the burdens.

- Don't be so focused *on* the trouble that you stop walking *through* the trouble. As you abide in the Lord and His Word abides in you, you will access all you need to live a life of enduring faith.

- Personal Notes:

## Application

Life gets hard, but a kingdom hero is a committed Christian who perseveres by faith in order to experience spiritual victory.

## Quotables

- Whatever battle you're in right now that's discouraging you and challenging you, others have fought, and they have come out winners. The witnesses want to give testimony that you can win too.

- I know you may be disappointed where you are. I know you may be unhappy where you are, but...I want you to look beyond where you are and thank God for where He's going to take you.

- God bless you as you start where you are, get up, keep going, because I think you're beginning to see your victory in sight.

## Video Group Discussion

1. Tony starts this final session by sharing how former champions are often paraded out at boxing matches to inspire both the crowd and the current fighters. Seeing people who have trained, fought, and won can give someone the courage they need to push harder than ever before. How does this illustration relate to our study of past kingdom heroes?

   Read Hebrews 12:1—"Since we have so great a cloud of witnesses surrounding us, let us also lay aside every encumbrance and the sin which so easily entangles us, and let us run with endurance the race that is set before us." Share about a time when someone's testimony encouraged or strengthened you in your own faith.

   What does it mean to "lay aside every encumbrance"?

   In what ways can an "encumbrance" keep someone from fully living a life of faith?

2. In the video, Tony describes how competitive swimmers will even shave off their body hair in order to remove anything and everything that could slow them down. This is an unusual thing to consider as an "encumbrance," but even hair can make the difference.

What are some unusual encumbrances that keep believers from living a life of faith? (Think outside the box.)

a.


b.


c.


What are some of the consequences of holding on to these encumbrances?

a.


b.


c.


3. Tony gives an illustration about watching the news while walking on the treadmill, comparing it to keeping your eyes on Jesus while walking forward in faith. While the two may not be apples to apples, how do they compare?




In your own words, describe what it means to keep your eyes focused on Jesus—especially in light of the reality that we cannot physically see Him.

Can you list one or more biblical examples of people who had to keep their eyes focused on Jesus in order to experience the fulfilment of their faith move?

Read Hebrews 12:2-3 together—"Fixing our eyes on Jesus, the author and perfecter of faith, who for the joy set before Him endured the cross, despising the shame, and has sat down at the right hand of the throne of God. For consider Him who has endured such hostility by sinners against Himself, so that you will not grow weary and lose heart." What does it mean to "lose heart"? How does that come across in practical, everyday actions?

What are some things losing heart can lead to in a person's life?

What does this passage encourage us to do in order to not grow weary or lose heart? In what ways can doing this help against things like burnout, bitterness, and apathy?

## Group Bible Exploration

1. Learning about kingdom heroes is a great way to inspire our own faith walk; in studying the lives of others or hearing the testimonies of others we gain a greater confidence along life's journey.

Read Hebrews 10:23-25—"Let us hold fast the confession of our hope without wavering, for He who promised is faithful; and let us consider how to stimulate one another to love and good deeds, not forsaking our own assembling together, as is the habit of some, but encouraging one another; and all the more as you see the day drawing near." In what ways do we forsake our own assembling together in contemporary culture?

What are some ways we can "stimulate one another to love and good deeds"?

What are some practical examples of "encouraging one another"?

How does the overall meaning of Hebrews 10:23-25 tie into our study on kingdom heroes of the faith?

2. Read together these two passages:

Philippians 1:20-21—"According to my earnest expectation and hope, that I will not be put to shame in anything, but that with all boldness, Christ will even now, as always, be exalted in my body, whether by life or by death. For to me, to live is Christ and to die is gain."

Hebrews 11:37-39—"They were stoned, they were sawn in two, they were tempted, they were put to death with the sword; they went about in sheepskins, in goat-skins, being destitute, afflicted, ill-treated (men of whom the world was not worthy), wandering in deserts and mountains and caves and holes in the ground. And all these, having gained approval through their faith, did not receive what was promised."

How does it make you feel to know that some rewards will not come until we reach heaven?

How does our culture's emphasis on instant gratification diminish the hope of obtaining future, eternal rewards?

What are some other ways Satan strategizes to get potential kingdom heroes off track?

3. Read together Hebrews 11:32-34:

What more shall I say? For time will fail me if I tell of Gideon, Barak, Samson, Jephthah, of David and Samuel and the prophets, who by faith conquered kingdoms, performed acts of righteousness, obtained promises, shut the mouths of lions, quenched the power of fire, escaped the edge of the sword, from weakness were made strong, became mighty in war, put foreign armies to flight.

What is your overall impression or thought about this passage?

Why do you think we don't see more people like Gideon, Barak, Samson, and David today?

In what ways are you seeking to learn from these great heroes of the faith and apply their life lessons to your life?

How do you feel when you've taken a step of faith—or even a leap of faith—and seen God's mighty hand work out something powerful?

## In Closing

As you end this study, remember these six things from our sessions:

1. Faith is the foundation to successfully running and finishing the race of life.

2. Worshipping by faith requires believing in God, knowing God, and adjusting your expectations to His. Authentic worship displays an honest faith and trust in God.

3. Choose to believe God's plan and act on it despite what the culture is saying, doing, or even pressuring you to do.

4. Your submission to God should push you to choose His wisdom over your own in your daily life.

5. You have to be willing to take the risk on God's Word to experience its worth.

6. Life gets hard, but a kingdom hero is a committed Christian who perseveres by faith in order to experience spiritual victory.

You have access to all the faith you need to fully live as a kingdom hero. It's up to you to choose to take the necessary steps of faith in your daily life decisions. Only you can take those steps; no one can do it for you. The faith walk is a personal, individual choice. The opportunity to live as a kingdom hero is available to you, but you must make the choices that reflect a life of faith to do so.

# THE URBAN ALTERNATIVE

The Urban Alternative (TUA) equips, empowers, and unites Christians to impact individuals, families, churches, and communities through a thoroughly kingdom-agenda worldview. In teaching truth, we seek to transform lives.

The core cause of the problems we face in our personal lives, homes, churches, and societies is a spiritual one. Therefore, the only way to address that core cause is spiritually. We've tried a political, social, economic, and even a religious agenda, and now it's time for a kingdom agenda.

*The kingdom agenda can be defined as the visible manifestation*
*of the comprehensive rule of God over every area of life.*

The unifying central theme throughout the Bible is the glory of God and the advancement of His kingdom. The conjoining thread from Genesis to Revelation—from beginning to end—is focused on one thing: God's glory through advancing God's kingdom.

When we do not recognize that theme, the Bible becomes for us a series of disconnected stories that are great for inspiration but seem to be unrelated in purpose and direction. Understanding the role of the kingdom in Scripture increases our understanding of the relevancy of this several-thousand-year-old text to our day-to-day living. That's because God's kingdom was not only then; it is now.

The absence of the kingdom's influence in our personal lives, family lives, churches, and communities has led to a deterioration in our world of immense proportions:

- People live segmented, compartmentalized lives because they lack God's kingdom worldview.

- Families disintegrate because they exist for their own satisfaction rather than for the kingdom.

- Churches are limited in the scope of their impact because they fail to comprehend that the goal of the church is not its existence but its influencing the world for the kingdom.

- Communities have nowhere to turn to find real solutions for real people who have real problems because the church has become divided, ingrown, and unable to transform the cultural and political landscape in any relevant way.

By optimizing the solutions of heaven, the kingdom agenda offers us a way to see and live life with a solid hope. When God is no longer the final and authoritative standard under which all else falls, order and hope have left with Him. But the reverse is true as well: If God is still in the picture, and as long as His agenda is still on the table, we have hope. Even if relationships collapse, God will sustain us. Even if finances dwindle, God will keep us. Even if dreams die, God will revive us. As long as God and His rule are still the overarching standard in our lives, families, churches, and communities, hope remains.

Our world needs the King's agenda. Our churches need the King's agenda. Our families need the King's agenda.

We've put together a three-part plan to direct us to heal the divisions and strive for unity as we move toward the goal of truly being one nation under God. This three-part plan calls us to assemble with others in unity, to address the issues that divide us, and to act together for social impact. Following this plan, we will see individuals, families, churches, and communities transformed as we follow God's kingdom agenda in every area of our lives. You can request this plan by emailing info@tonyevans.org or by going online to tonyevans.org.

In many major cities, drivers can take a loop to the other side of the city when they don't want to head straight through downtown. This loop takes them close enough to the city center so they can see its towering buildings and skyline but not close enough to actually experience it.

This is precisely what we, as a culture, have done with God. We have put Him on the "loop" of our personal, family, church, and community lives. He's close enough to be at hand should we need Him in an emergency but far enough away that He can't be the center of who we are. We want God on the "loop," not the King of the Bible who comes downtown into the very heart of our ways. And as we have seen in our own lives and in the lives of others, leaving God on the "loop" brings about dire consequences.

But when we make God and His rule the centerpiece of all we think, do, or say, we experience Him in the way He longs for us to experience Him. He wants us to be kingdom people with kingdom minds set on fulfilling His kingdom's purposes. He wants us to pray, as Jesus did, "Not my will, but Thy will be done" because His is the kingdom, the power, and the glory.

There is only one God, and we are not Him. As King and Creator, God calls the shots. Only when we align ourselves under His comprehensive hand do we access His full power and authority in all spheres of life: personal, familial, ecclesiastical, and government.

As we learn how to govern ourselves under God, we then transform the institutions of family, church, and society using a biblically based kingdom worldview.

*Under Him, we touch heaven and change earth.*

To achieve our goal, we use a variety of strategies, approaches, and resources for reaching and equipping as many people as possible.

## Broadcast Media

Millions of individuals experience *The Alternative with Dr. Tony Evans*, a daily broadcast on nearly 1,400 radio outlets and in over 130 countries. The broadcast can also be seen on several television networks and is available online at tonyevans.org. As well, you can listen to or view the daily broadcast by downloading the Tony Evans app for free in the App Store. Over 30,000,000 message downloads/streams occur each year.

## Leadership Training

The *Tony Evans Training Center* (TETC) facilitates a comprehensive discipleship platform, which provides an educational program that embodies the ministry philosophy of Dr. Tony Evans as expressed through the kingdom agenda. The training courses focus on leadership development and discipleship in the following five tracks:

- Bible & Theology
- Personal Growth
- Family and Relationships
- Church Health and Leadership Development
- Society and Community Impact Strategies

The TETC program includes courses for both local and online students. Furthermore, TETC programming includes course work for non-student attendees. Pastors, Christian leaders, and Christian laity—both local and at a distance—can seek out the Kingdom Agenda Certificate for personal, spiritual, and professional development. For more information, visit tonyevanstraining.org.

*Kingdom Agenda Pastors* (KAP) provides a viable network for like-minded pastors who embrace the kingdom agenda philosophy. Pastors have the opportunity to go deeper with Dr. Tony Evans as they are given greater biblical knowledge, practical applications, and resources to impact individuals, families, churches, and communities. KAP welcomes senior and associate pastors of all churches. KAP also offers an annual KAP Summit each year in Dallas with intensive seminars, workshops, and resources. For more information, visit: kafellowship.org

*Pastors' Wives Ministry*, founded by Dr. Lois Evans, provides counsel, encouragement, and spiritual resources for pastors' wives as they serve with their husbands in the ministry. A primary focus of the ministry is the KAP Summit, where senior pastors' wives are offered a safe place to reflect, renew, and relax, along with training in personal development, spiritual growth, and care for their emotional and physical well-being. For more information, visit loisevans.org.

## Kingdom Community Impact

The outreach programs of The Urban Alternative seek to provide positive impact on individuals, churches, families, and communities through a variety of ministries. We see these efforts as necessary to our calling as a ministry and essential to the communities we serve. With training on how to initiate and maintain programs to adopt schools; provide homeless services; and partner toward unity and justice with the local police precincts, which creates a connection between the police and our community, we, as a ministry, live out God's kingdom agenda according to our *Kingdom Strategy for Community Transformation*.

The *Kingdom Strategy for Community Transformation* is a three-part plan that equips churches to have a positive impact on their communities for the kingdom of God. It also provides numerous practical suggestions for how this three-part plan can be implemented in your community, and it serves as a blueprint for unifying churches around the common goal of creating a better world for all of us. For more information, visit tonyevans.org, then click on the link to access the 3-Point Plan.

The *National Church Adopt-a-School Initiative* (NCAASI) prepares churches across the country to impact communities by using public schools as the primary vehicle for effecting positive social change in urban youth and families. Leaders of churches, school districts, faith-based organizations, and other nonprofit organizations are equipped with the knowledge and tools to forge partnerships and build strong social service delivery systems. This training is based on the comprehensive church-based community impact strategy conducted by Oak Cliff Bible Fellowship. It addresses such areas as economic development, education, housing, health revitalization, family renewal, and racial reconciliation. We assist churches in tailoring the model to meet specific needs of their communities while simultaneously addressing the spiritual and moral frame of reference. Training events are held annually in the Dallas area at Oak Cliff Bible Fellowship. For more information, visit churchadoptaschool.org.

*Athlete's Impact* (AI) exists as an outreach both into and through the sports arena. Coaches can be the most influential factor in young people's lives, even ahead of their parents. With the growing rise of fatherlessness in our culture, more young people are looking to their coaches for guidance, character development, meeting practical needs, and hope. Athletes fall just after coaches on the influencer scale. Whether professional or amateur, they influence younger athletes and kids within their spheres of impact. Knowing this, we aim to equip and train coaches and athletes on how to live out and utilize their God-given roles for the benefit of the kingdom. We aim to do this through our iCoach App as well as through resources such as *The Playbook: A Life Strategy Guide for Athletes.* For more information, visit icoachapp.org.

*Tony Evans Films* ushers in positive life change through compelling video-shorts, animation, and feature-length films. We seek to build kingdom disciples through the power of story; use a variety of platforms for viewer consumption and have more than 100,000,000 digital views; and merge video-shorts and film with relevant Bible study materials to bring people to the saving knowledge of Jesus Christ and to strengthen the body of Christ worldwide. Tony Evans Films released its first feature-length film, *Kingdom Men Rising*, in April 2019 in over 800 theaters nationwide and in partnership with Lifeway Films. The second release, *Journey with Jesus*, is in partnership with RightNow Media.

## Resource Development

By providing a variety of published materials, we are fostering lifelong learning partnerships with the people we serve. Dr. Evans has authored more than 125 unique titles based on over 50 years of preaching—in booklet, book, or Bible-study format. He also holds the honor of writing the first full-Bible commentary by an African American. *The Tony Evans Study Bible* was released in 2019, and it sits in permanent display as a historic release in the Museum of the Bible in Washington, D.C.

For more information and a complimentary copy of Dr. Evans's devotional newsletter, call (800) 800-3222; write to TUA at P.O. Box 4000, Dallas, TX, 75208; or visit us online at:

## www.TonyEvans.org

# TonyEVANS
## THE URBAN ALTERNATIVE

YOUR *Eternity* IS OUR *Priority*

At The Urban Alternative, eternity is our priority—for the individual, the family, the church and the nation. The 45-year teaching ministry of Tony Evans has allowed us to reach a world in need with:

**The Alternative** – Our flagship radio program brings hope and comfort to an audience of millions on over 1,300 radio outlets across the country.

**tonyevans.org** – Our library of teaching resources provides solid Bible teaching through the inspirational books and sermons of Tony Evans.

**Tony Evans Training Center** – Experience the adventure of God's Word with our online classroom, providing at-your-own-pace courses for your PC or mobile device.

**Tony Evans app** – Packed with audio and video clips, devotionals, Scripture readings and dozens of other tools, the mobile app provides inspiration on-the-go.

**Explore God's kingdom today.**
**Live for more than the moment.**
**Live for *eternity*.**

tonyevans.org